Piano • Vocal • Guitar

Lynyrd Skynyrd
GREATEST HITS

MW00989238

CONTENTS

ISBN 0-634-09209-X

HAL•LEONARD®
CORPORATION
7777 W. BLUEMOUND RD. P.O. BOX 13819 MILWAUKEE, WI 53213

Visit Hal Leonard Online at
www.halleonard.com

THE BALLAD OF CURTIS LOEW

Words and Music by ALLEN COLLINS
and RONNIE VAN ZANT

Slowly

Well, I used to wake the morn - in' be -

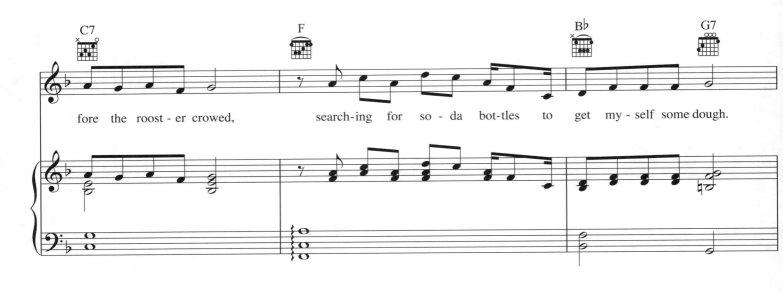

fore the roost - er crowed, search-ing for so - da bot-tles to get my - self some dough.

Brought 'em down to the cor - ner, __ down to the coun - try store; __

'cause Cur - tis Loew was the fin - est pick - er to

ev - er play ___ the blues.

ev - er play ___ the blues.   ev - er play ___ the blues.

rit.

CALL ME THE BREEZE

Words and Music by
JOHN CALE

chang - es in me.
keep mov - in' on.
feel right at home.

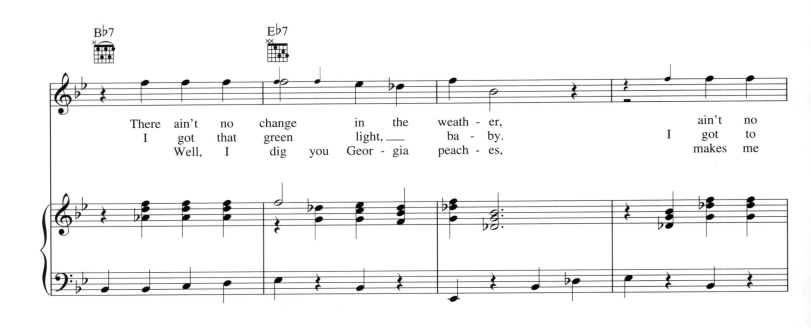

There ain't no change in the weath - er, ain't no
I got that green light, ___ ba - by. I got to
Well, I dig you Geor - gia peach - es, makes me

chang - es in me.
keep mov - in' on.
feel right at home.

COMIN' HOME

Words and Music by ALLEN COLLINS
and RONNIE VAN ZANT

Moderately

It's been so long __ since I've __ been gone. __ An-oth-er day __ might be too long __ for me. __

Trav - 'lin a -round I've had my fill. _____ Bro - ken dreams_ and dirt - y deals. _

Con - crete jun - gle sur -round -ing me. _____ Man - y nights_ I've slept out in the

12

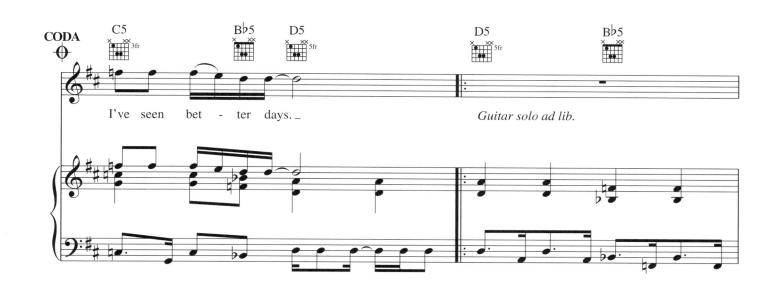

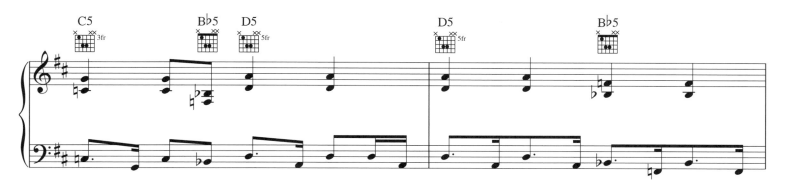

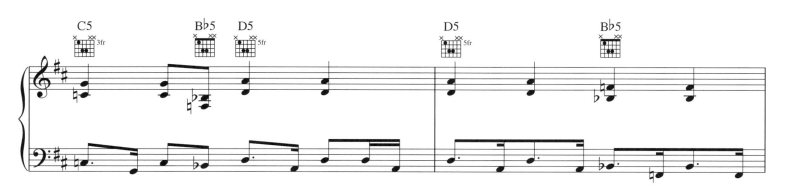

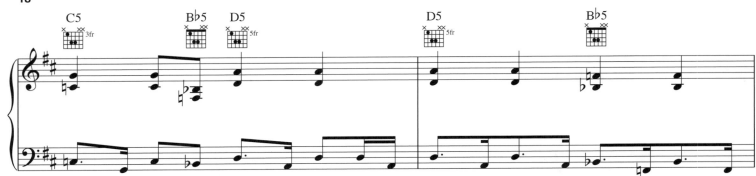

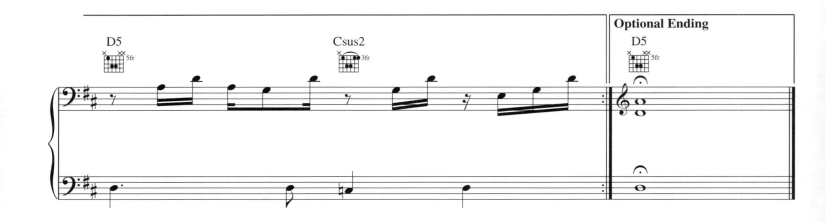

DON'T ASK ME NO QUESTIONS

Words and Music by RONNIE VAN ZANT
and GARY ROSSINGTON

Well, ev-'ry time that I ____ come home ___ no-bod-

-y wants to leave me be. ____ It seems that all the

friends I've got ___ just got ___ to come in-ter-ro-gate me.

DOUBLE TROUBLE

Words and Music by ALLEN COLLINS
and RONNIE VAN ZANT

Moderately, with a beat

28

FREE BIRD

Words and Music by ALLEN COLLINS
and RONNIE VAN ZANT

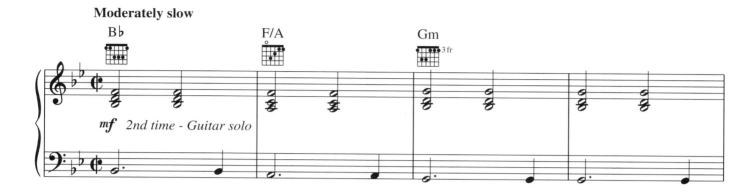

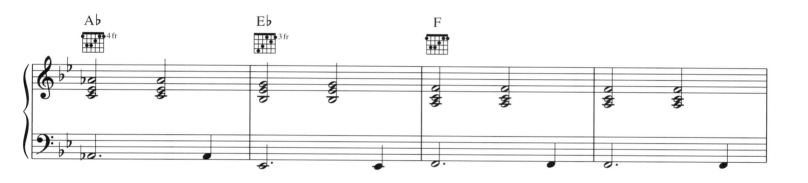

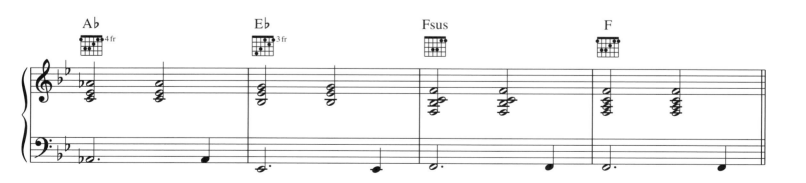

DOWN SOUTH JUKIN'

Words and Music by RONNIE VAN ZANT
and GARY ROSSINGTON

Well Bil- ly Joe told me, said a ev- 'ry- thing's_ look- in' fine._

Now put your Sun-day pants on, let's get out ___ on the road. ___ We been work-in' all week and I think ___ that it's time ___ we let go. ___ We got a three fine mam-mas sit-tin' all a-lone. _ Gon-na

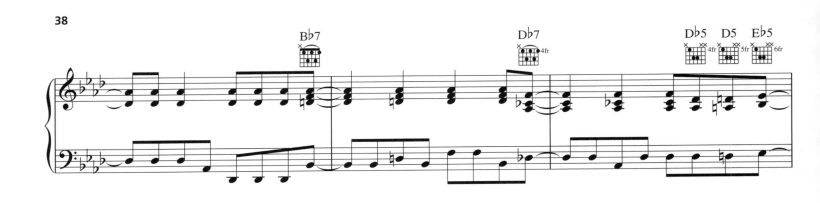

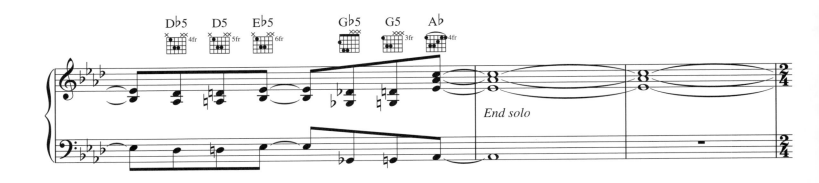

Now come Mon-day morn-in' we're head-ed back to the fields ___

___ and we'll be do-in' our thing for Pa-

GIMME BACK MY BULLETS

Words and Music by GARY ROSSINGTON
and RONNIE VAN ZANT

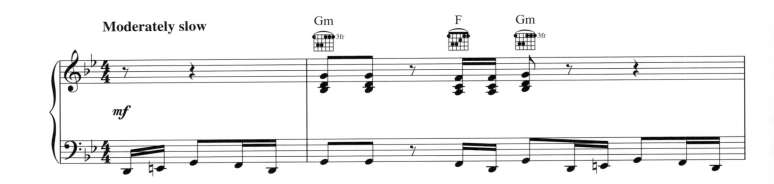

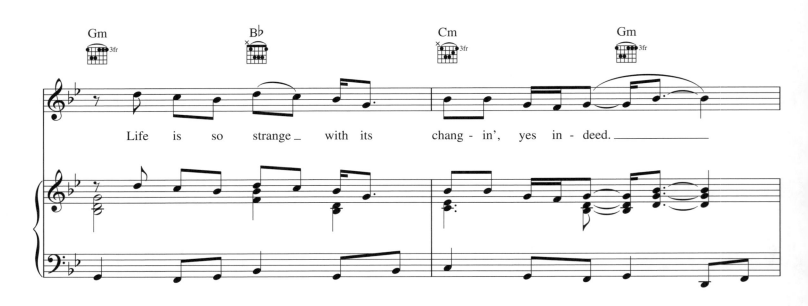

Life is so strange _ with its chang-in', yes in-deed. ____

GIMME THREE STEPS

Words and Music by ALLEN COLLINS
and RONNIE VAN ZANT

I AIN'T THE ONE

Words and Music by GARY ROSSINGTON
and RONNIE VAN ZANT

move a - long, __ I do be - lieve. ___

End Instrumental

I KNOW A LITTLE

Words and Music by
STEVE EARL GAINES

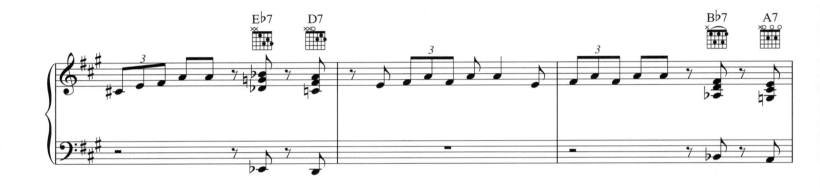

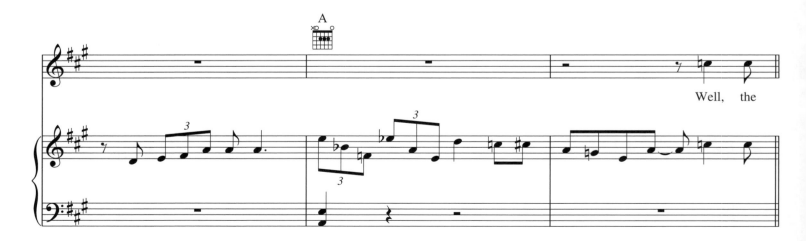

Well, the

53

THE NEEDLE AND THE SPOON

Words and Music by ALLEN COLLINS
and RONNIE VAN ZANT

Thir- ty days Lord and
I've been feel-ing so
I've seen a lot of peo-ple who

thir-ty nights ___
sick in-side, ___
thought they were cool ___

I'm com-ing home on an
got to get bet-ter, Lord, be-
but then a- gain, Lord, I've

ON THE HUNT

Words and Music by ALLEN COLLINS
and RONNIE VAN ZANT

SATURDAY NIGHT SPECIAL

Words and Music by EDWARD KING
and RONNIE VAN ZANT

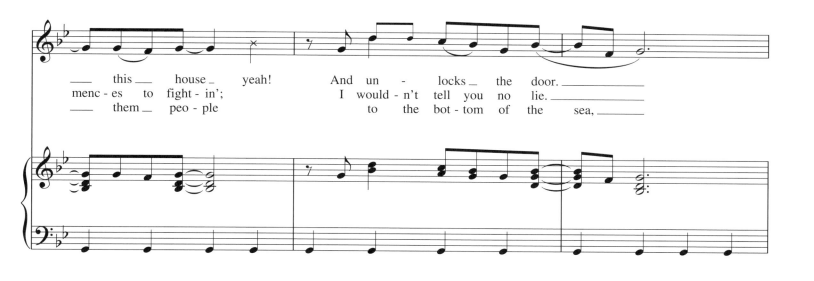

_____ this _____ house _____ yeah! And un - locks _____ the door. _____
menc - es to fight - in'; I would - n't tell you no lie. _____
_____ them _____ peo - ple to the bot - tom of the sea, _____

And as a man's reach-ing for his trou - sers, shoots him full of thir -
And big _____ Jim done _____ pulled his pis - tol, shot his friend right _____
be - fore some fool come a - round _____ here wan - na shoot ei - ther _____

C   Gm

- ty eight holes. _____
_____ be - tween the eyes.   }   It's the Sat - ur - day night _____ spe - cial
_____ you or me. _____

SWEET HOME ALABAMA

Words and Music by RONNIE VAN ZANT,
ED KING and GARY ROSSINGTON

69

THAT SMELL

Words and Music by RONNIE VAN ZANT
and ALLEN COLLINS

Driving Rock

Whis-key bot - tles _____ and brand_ new cars; _____
An - gel of dark - ness is up - on _____ you,
One lit - tle prob - lem that con-fronts _____ you,

To Coda

The smell of death sur - rounds ___ you. _____

Now they call you ___ Prince

Charm - ing. __   Can't speak a word _ when you're full of 'ludes. _

Say you'll be all - right come to-mor - row, _   but to - mor-row   might not be here ___ for you. _

WHAT'S YOUR NAME

Words and Music by GARY ROSSINGTON
and RONNIE VAN ZANT

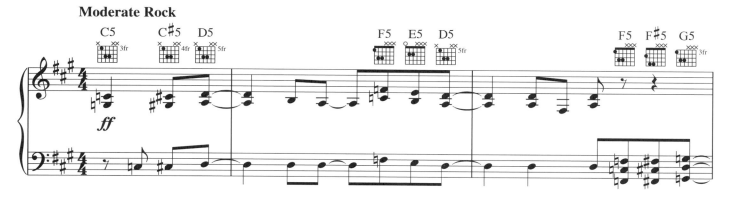

Well it's eight o'- clock _ in Boi-

-se, I - da - ho. ___ I find my

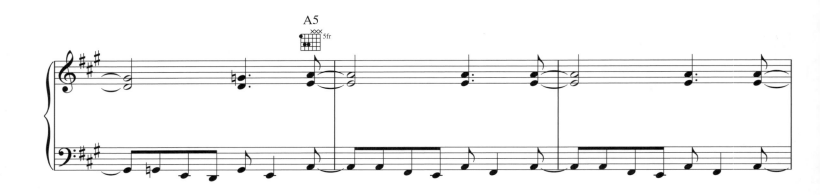

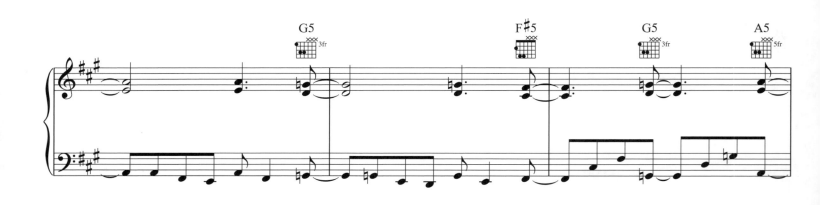

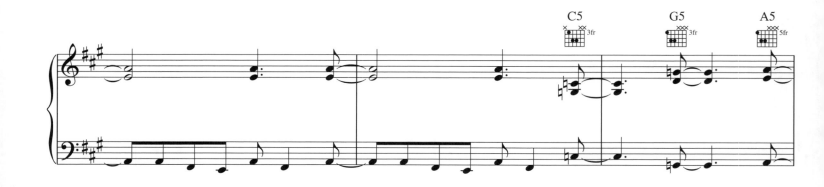

TUESDAY'S GONE

Words and Music by ALLEN COLLINS
and RONNIE VAN ZANT

WHISKEY ROCK-A-ROLLER

Words and Music by EDWARD KING,
RONNIE VAN ZANT and BILLIE POWELL

Lyrics:

I'm head-ed down the high-way, got my suit-case by my side.
I was born a trav-'lin' man and my feets do burn the ground.
Instrumental
Take me down to Mem-phis town, bus driv-er get me there.

A blue sky's hang-ing o-ver my head, I got five
I don't care for fan-cy mu-sic if your shoes
I got me a queen-ie she got long

YOU GOT THAT RIGHT

Words and Music by STEVE EARL GAINES
and RONNIE VAN ZANT

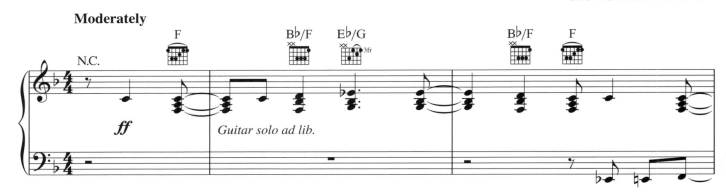

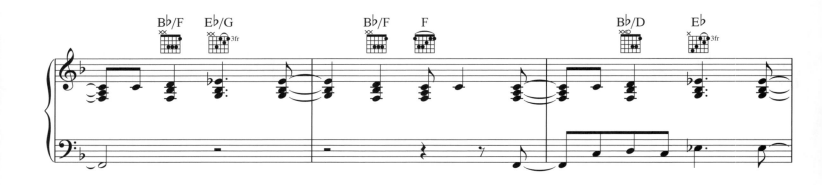

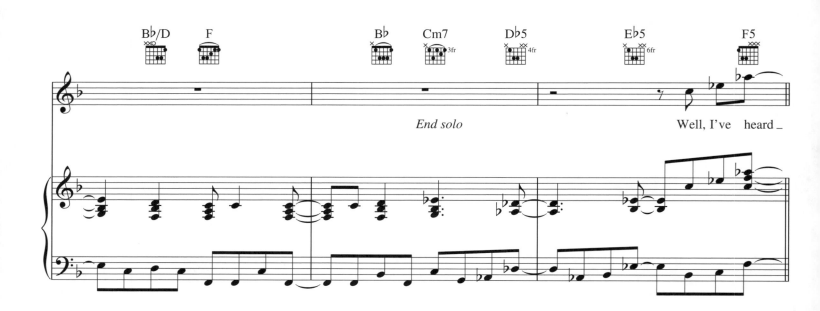

Guitar solo ad lib.

Well, you got that right. _____

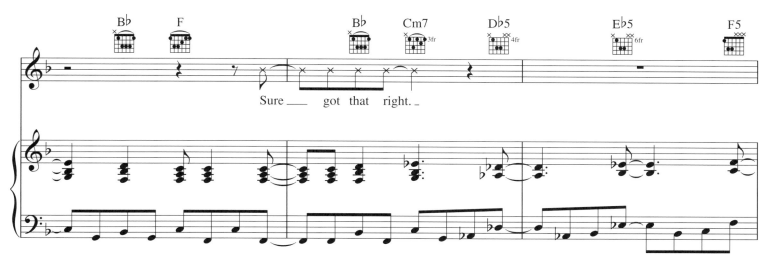

Sure ___ got that right. _

Guitar solo ad lib.